CAPTAIN OATES' LEFT SOCK

A play

JOHN ANTROBUS

Copyright © 1974 by John Antrobus
All Rights Reserved

CAPTAIN OATES' LEFT SOCK is fully protected under the copyright laws of the British Commonwealth, including Canada, the United States of America, and all other countries of the Copyright Union. All rights, including professional and amateur stage productions, recitation, lecturing, public reading, motion picture, radio broadcasting, television and the rights of translation into foreign languages are strictly reserved.

ISBN 978-0-573-01701-8

www.samuelfrench.co.uk
www.samuelfrench.com

For Amateur Production Enquiries

United Kingdom and World excluding North America

plays@samuelfrench.co.uk
020 7255 4302/01

Each title is subject to availability from Samuel French, depending upon country of performance.

CAUTION: Professional and amateur producers are hereby warned that *CAPTAIN OATES' LEFT SOCK* is subject to a licensing fee. Publication of this play does not imply availability for performance. Both amateurs and professionals considering a production are strongly advised to apply to the appropriate agent before starting rehearsals, advertising, or booking a theatre. A licensing fee must be paid whether the title is presented for charity or gain and whether or not admission is charged.

The professional rights in this play are controlled by Samuel French Ltd, 24-32 Stephenson Way, London, NW1 2HD.

No one shall make any changes in this title for the purpose of production. No part of this book may be reproduced, stored in a retrieval system, or transmitted in any form, by any means, now known or yet to be invented, including mechanical, electronic, photocopying, recording, videotaping, or otherwise, without the prior written permission of the publisher. No one shall upload this title, or part of this title, to any social media websites.

The right of John Antrobus to be identified as author of this work has been asserted in accordance with Section 77 of the Copyright, Designs and Patents Act 1988.

CAPTAIN OATES' LEFT SOCK

First presented as a Sunday night production at the Royal Court Theatre, London, on the 6th July 1969, and subsequently at the Theatre Upstairs on the 16th April 1973

Cast for the Theatre Upstairs production:

Dr Parks	Matthew Guiness
Carter	Nicholas Selby
Molly Topps	Gabrielle Daye
David	Stephen Rea
Celia	Janet Webb
Juliet	Margaret Brady
Nurse Bryant	Carol Macready
Margaret	Judith Paris
Nurse Rogers	James Donnelly
The Colonel	Geoffrey Edwards
Dorothy	Jill Richards
Fergy	Oliver Cotton
William	Martin Skinner
Rose	Jenny Tomasin
A Newcomer	Charles Kinross

The play directed by Nicholas Wright
Setting by Harriet Geddes

The action passes in the reception room of a psychiatric clinic

Time—the present

AUTHOR'S NOTE

It is most important that there are no lighting effects for this play. For instance, if you came to a public meeting you would not expect lights to dim and certain people to be highlighted. On the other hand you would not expect your attention to wander because the person talking was not spotlighted. Your attention might wander for other reasons. To let the significance of this play come through it must be staged in a very untheatrical way. The patients are ordinary people, and the doctor and nurses who dress in the same way, that is in a way that compliments their own personality, are like them. There should be no tendencies to suggest bedlam. Here are ordinary people in a state of distress, met together. If possible stage the play in the round — a circle of chairs in the middle — with the audience sitting all round. Let the cast make their entrances in the same manner as the audience enter, so that one may well ask "who are the sick?" Between group meetings the patients may rise, and move around, and possibly sit in different chairs. This does present differing views of the cast to the audience. But they should certainly not all exit and enter for each meeting. The flow of the play must be kept light. And if the cast re-arrange themselves let them do so as if informally.

CAPTAIN OATES' LEFT SOCK

A clinic reception room

Doctor Parks enters and addresses the audience

Parks I'm Doctor Hugh Parks—not that it matters—Tales of the Old National Health Service—now it can be told—sort of thing—the adventures of modern psychiatry—standing on the frontier of the mind—new lands—vast—madness—no—an innocent term, but see what I mean—must clean those shoes—irrelevant—arrogant—innocent I meant as an unformed attitude to the problem. You think we shut 'em in and lock'em up and is there any madness in the family—stigma—can't look the employer in the face—you mean you live near one of those places—aren't you frightened for your children? They should be tattooed on their foreheads as some sort of warning—not left to roam the streets—visit tobacconists—converse—fool the public by behaviour that can only be described as normal—normal—funny term, that—normal—have they dropped the bomb yet—I suppose normal people who dropped the bomb wouldn't care that it dropped on the insane—you don't get my point—get on with the story—if you won't go. I was resident psychiatrist at Newmown Clinic . . .

As Parks speaks the Patients enter and sit in the circle of chairs. They are Carter, a middle-aged man who fidgets; Molly Topps, a woman of about sixty; David, a young man; Celia, fat and thirty; the Colonel, elderly; Juliet, in her early twenties; Margaret, thin, anxious, still pretty but looking very run down, she is thirty-five; Dorothy, who is not pretty and a bit lumpy, thirty; Fergy, a seedy music student; William and Rose, the youngest in the group, both about eighteen

A few years previously it was known as Debbington House—they keep changing the name as it gets a reputation for being a nut-house—look here, one of my patients was run over by you lot—left alone he might have committed suicide in his own time . . .

Nurse Bryant and Nurse Rogers enter and join the circle. Nurse Bryant is a woman of twenty-six, hefty but not plain. Rogers is a middle-aged male nurse
(Indicating Carter) That one—that's Carter—fidget, fidget—arrange the next fag in the packet . . .
Carter carefully arranges a packet of cigarettes, matches, ashtray
A tidy world—secure. (He indicates Molly) and that's . . .

Molly   *(speaking towards the empty chair where Parks will sit)* I wish to know the date of my discharge, Doctor—you promised me—the date of my discharge . . .
Doctor Parks sits in his chair

First Group Meeting

Parks   *(to the audience)* Ten patients—staff nurse—male—female—can you tell the difference? All in mufti—civvies . . .

Molly   You promised you would tell me when I was well enough to leave the hospital.
Silence

Parks   *(in the scene)* Perhaps you should ask the group.

David   Now come on, we're not qualified for that—thats your job—are we supposed to discharge ourselves?
Parks does not answer. Silence

Molly   He promised—the doctor did promise—to tell me when I was well enough to leave—I want to know.

David   It's only fair—he thinks you know when you're well enough . .

Celia   Should we?

David   What?

Celia   Should we know when we're well enough?

David   That's the doctors job—surely we do enough of their work—sitting here—analyzing each other all day—I mean fair enough . . .

Celia   I mean . . .

David   Wait a minute—I mean we're not qualified—to tell each other our ailments . .

Celia   But don't you . .

CAPTAIN OATES' LEFT SOCK

David	Shut—shut up a minute . . .
Carter	I say . . .
David	We are not qualified—they sit there—doctors—they say nothing . . .
Carter	I say . . .
Molly	I think this group thing is bad—very bad—I'm sorry doctor I do—you won't even tell me now what you promised.
Celia	Do you feel better—Molly?
Molly	Oh yes I feel wonderful—thanks to the doctor—they've all been wonderful—I can't thank them enough—I want to get down on my knees . . .
Carter	I say . . .
Molly	And pray—pray—wonderful . . .
Carter	David—you showed emotion—you told Celia to shut up—is that because she stirs revulsion in you—do regard her—sorry, Celia—as a sow—an ever fertile ever reproducing cow?
David	No.
Carter	Oh . . .
Celia	Why do you call me a sow Mr Carter? Why? Why? What have I done—eh please, tell me—to deserve that?
Carter	I called David—that is Celia I asked David if he regarded you in that way—as a sort of revolting nature symbol . . .
David	It came from your lips . . .
Carter	I did not call Celia an ever reproducing sow—with big tappies . . .
Celia	What?
Molly	Oh dear—Mr Carter . . .
Celia	Big tappies . . .
David	He means your paps . . .
Celia	Oh—you make me feel like—like—I don't know—like . . .
Colonel	An ever—reproducing cow—sorry, sow . . .
Celia	I don't mind . . .
	Silence
Juliet	Perhaps you are jealous?
Carter	What? I beg your pardon, Juliet?

Juliet	I mean of—Celia's reproducing system ...
Carter	Now why should you say that—it never crossed my mind—why should I want to reproduce—there's enough of you—oh dear no ...
Nurse Bryant	Mr Carter—excuse me ...
Carter	Certainly Nurse Bryant—say what you will ...
Nurse Bryant	Why did you say tappies?
Carter	Did I say tappies? I thought I said paps ...
Celia	David said paps ...
Carter	Why did you say paps David?
Nurse Bryant	You're avoiding my question Mr. Carter ...
Carter	One never knows—these things can be turned on in the rush hour I suppose—no offence ...
Celia	Oh I don't mind—if it helps you to talk about my body.
Carter	I don't wish to—I don't think it would help your mind ..
David	It might help yours. Surely we were discussing Molly's discharge ...
Molly	I would like to know—doctor surely you should say something ...
Parks	How do you feel?
Molly	I feel wonderful—I could go down on my knees—wonderful—wonderful ...
David	If there's no doubt why can't you say I'm ready to leave the hospital ...
Molly	Surely that's the doctor's job—not mine—it would be wrong ...
Carter	Wrong ...
Molly	Wrong of me to say I felt well ...
Carter	You said it ...
David	You did say it ...
Molly	But he should know, the doctor ...
Carter	In fact Molly you don't trust yourself—you might still be very shaky ...
Molly	Oh no—wonderful—wonderful—I've never felt better—really.

CAPTAIN OATES' LEFT SOCK

Carter	But you don't trust your own diagnosis . . .
Molly	I don't—need to—it's his job—I thank you, Doctor—I do thank Doctor Parks so much—so very much—I just want him to tell me when I can go home . . .
David	He should—he should tell you that . . .
Molly	You get no privacy—I mean all these group meetings—you never get the doctor on his own . . .
Margaret	I feel that—I mean they tell you nothing. I mean, why should we discuss your personal problem in front of others—not qualified . . .
David	What problem?
Margaret	Oh there's nothing wrong with me—I just want to get well . . I mean get better—there's nothing wrong—I just want to feel well and get home—I don't feel well . .
Parks	But there's nothing wrong with you?
Margaret	No—not really. The ECT makes me feel unwell . . .
David	I think it's damn primitive—tying electrodes to your head—shocking you—can't they do better than that? It's cruel . . .
Molly	I felt wonderful after my ECT . . .
David	She doesn't—there doesn't seem to be treatment—here . . nothing you can put your finger on . . .
Molly	Oh I feel wonderful—I felt so awful when I arrived . . .
David	But what's happening—we sit round talking all day—I mean all right, Celia's got paps—but talking about that all day—and alternatively—with it I mean—a few shocks for some—ECT . . .
Nurse Bryant	Perhaps its doing Mr Carter good to talk about Celia's tappies.
Rogers	Perhaps you'd prefer him to talk about your tappies, Nurse . .
Carter	Oh come on—I've got—I mean I see no point in embarrassing people—Celia's body—its the mind we must cure—damn the body—damn the body . . .
Nurse Bryant	Why?
Carter	I beg your pardon?
Nurse Bryant	Why damn the body?

Carter	Oh that's very clever—that's all very well—oh my goodness I know the interelation between genes and the mind—the chemical balance—disturbed—can produce in the mind alarming symptoms. Oh yes I know—we know that surely—but that surely is between doctor and patient—an analysis— chemical which we can't make—I mean its all very well—the group is not given the keys to the pill cupboard—nor should that be so . . .
David	It wouldn't surprise me—why not go the whole hog—hand the lot over to us—the patients—either one thing or the other—we might as well bodge the whole lot—why after years of training Doctor Parks should sit there in silence . . silence . . .
Parks	Silence—a fair accusation—but—on the frontiers—one dreams . . . Cure—cure—the nub—cure—imp . . . Cure what—why? Never mind how. Celia's tappies . . . another day . . .

Second Group Meeting

Celia	A pink slip of mine has gone missing, that's two in three days.
Carter	Pink?
Celia	Oh yes, Mr Carter—both pink . . .
Margaret	Yes, I lost one from the laundry room—yesterday . . .
David	Why should the men and the women share the same laundry room?
Carter	Oh yes . . .
David	It doesn't seem right . .
Carter	David, there's no harm in that—we're not sex maniacs—if we can't trust each other with each other's laundry . . .
Colonel	Obviously not . .
Celia	I'm not accusing anybody—please don't think that . . .
David	It makes me sick—I mean a deliberate sharing of a facility . . .
Carter	Are you against mixed facilities?
David	No—I mean where to draw the line—we share the music room—all right, all right—cards, record player—dining-room—company—but we can't sleep together, can we—so why should we be forced to share a promiscuous facility?

CAPTAIN OATES' LEFT SOCK

Carter	I like that phrase young David—I really do—I can see no harm in it—it adds warmth and charm to the facilities—after all . .
Celia	But why should my pink slip go missing?
Carter	Who knew it was yours? Whoever took it? Who would know? Oh hell, Celia I beg your pardon—but you seem to take it personally . . .
Celia	It was my slip—pink . . .
Margaret	And mine—whoever took it . . .
David	Could be the doctors—what—to bring stress on the group pressure—we are forced to share a facility like that—then item by item they build up the pressure—who the hell knows what sort of treatment we're getting in this place . . .
Molly	Are you suggesting the doctors took the two pink slips—oh I don't think that—they've been so wonderful—wonderful . . .
Carter	Why pink? Pink? What can that hide?
Rogers	Pardon?
Carter	Pardon?
Rogers	Hide? You said hide?
Carter	Motive . .
Rogers	The pink slip hides the motive . . .
David	And the body . .
Juliet	Perhaps Mr Carter would like the pink slip to hide his body?
Carter	My dear Juliet—come on now—I am old enough to be your father—if I want a pink slip I will away and buy my own—I would certainly not want—not that I want a slip—but oh no— I would not wish to borrow Celia's slip whatever colour it was. Not that I have anything to do with slips . . .
David	Especially not Celia's?
Carter	Precisely . . . I don't see that you're talking about . .
	Silence
Parks	The Colonel seems to be falling asleep . . .
Colonel	*(opening his eyes)* I assumed the subject was exhausted . . .
David	Perhaps we should turn out our lockers?

Colonel	I don't mind—I'm sure you'll find nothing of interest in mine...
Celia	Perhaps in the general interests of the group I can launch an appeal—please—please—anyone—return the slips—and we'll all be happy...
David	Except the person who retuns them...
Celia	Eh?
David	How can you tell? If we have a laundry stealer in our midst then surely this is a symptom—we need a confession...
Celia	I don't wish to embarrass anyone...
Carter	But you do, Celia?
Celia	How? Please tell me how? And I'll do what I can to stop it...
Carter	It's too late...
Nurse Bryant	You said that with a certain amount of antagonism...
Carter	I just said it's much too late...
Nurse Bryant	What for?
Carter	My dear Nurse Bryant, surely it is much too late not to discuss a problem that we have just finished discussing—that's all...
Nurse Bryant	That causes you embarrassment...
Carter	No certainly not—I am willing to talk about anything—to co-operate fully—that's why we are here—to find out—heaven knows what...
Nurse Bryant	And yet you were embarrassed—surely that's interesting..
Carter	I said that Celia may have been—that is that is much too late for Celia not to be embarrassing...
David	She must have been embarrassing someone...
Celia	I'm sorry, I really am. I don't want to—I want to help...if someone is really, really in need of my slip—please, please keep it...
Nurse Bryant	You are frowning, Mr. Carter.
Carter	I will gladly turn out my locker Nurse Bryant—to oblige—to oblige...

CAPTAIN OATES' LEFT SOCK

Juliet	You might be wearing the slip—Mr Carter . . .
Carter	Two slips? How could I get them on under my trousers?
Colonel	*(laughing)* Fascinating . . .
Carter	Oh yes . . .
Colonel	The problem . . .
Carter	I know—am I Houdini . . .
Molly	Oh really—perhaps they blew away . . .
David	What?
Molly	In the wind . . .
David	What wind?
Molly	The window open . . .
David	We haven't had any wind for days . . .
Carter	It was blowing a gale last night . . .
David	No . . .
Margaret	Very windy . . .
Celia	Before we went to bed, that would only account for one slip.
David	All right it was windy—a gale—eh yes but why a gale should just blow out of the window pink—pink slips . . .
Colonel	*(laughing)* A good point . . .
	Silence
Parks	Dorothy has not said anything for three days . . .
	Dorothy is still in gesture, nerves seizing up her joints, as she rubs her hands together.
Molly	She said a nice lot of things at breakfast—she spoke very well.
David	What about?
Molly	Oh yes—the toast.
David	That's a start . . .
Molly	Oh yes—we must be thankful for small mercies . . .
Parks	Can you say anything to us today, Dorothy?
	Dorothy just rubs her hands together
Molly	I think she's a bit upset today, Doctor—are you Dorothy? Yes she is—she's a bit upset . . .
David	What about, the toast?
Molly	No—oh no David of course not—she had a visit from her parents yesterday, didn't you Dorothy? Yes, she did.

Parks	Did you find this upsetting Dorothy?
	Dorothy rubs her hands together
	Can you tell us, Dorothy, how you felt upset? What upsets you?
	Dorothy rubs her hands together
David	Stubborn...
Molly	Oh no. Dorothy, how did your parents upset you yesterday? Doctor Parks would like to know.
David	We all would...
Molly	Doctor Parks said, how did they upset you, Dorothy—can you try and tell us?
	Dorothy rubs her hands
	No—no—she's a bit distressed today—aren't you? I said, you're distressed today. Yes—yes—they said something about your brother, didn't they—yes, they did. Yes—what was it they said, now—he's re-decorated her room—hasn't he, Dot—Dorothy—in pink...
David	Pink?
Molly	She doesn't like pink.
David	She doesn't like pink—it's all coming out now...
	Dorothy rubs her hands together. Silence
Parks	*(to the audience)* Then there was Ferguson—Fergy—musician—student training. Not said much—till he surfaced one day...

Third Group Meeting

Fergy	I feel I should make a decision...
David	What?
Fergy	A decision—decide—make up my mind...
David	What about?
Fergy	I don't know—I'm not sure—that's the first step. I feel I'm able to make decisions now—after all this time—say about Molly—she can be discharged.
Molly	Do you think so?
Fergy	Without a doubt.
Molly	I'd rather hear it from the Doctor.
Fergy	Don't you trust me?
Molly	He's qualified.

CAPTAIN OATES' LEFT SOCK

Fergy	Yes—no—yes—what's the use—I make a decision—wrong— or right—and he decides—the Doctor—this throws me . . .
David	Would you like to discharge Molly?
Fergy	I could do—if I was in charge . . .
Colonel	Why should someone be in charge . . . *(He laughs)*
Molly	Surely that's the Doctor's job—we all admire and respect him . . .
Fergy	Another thing—sorry . . .
Molly	Go on . . .
Fergy	I'm sorry . . .
Molly	Don't apologize Fergy . . .
David	Let him apologize . . .
Fergy	I don't know what I'm apologizing for—I'm sorry. I want to come to a decision about myself—today I feel I can—I could climb mountains—percussion or brass . . .
Molly	This has been troubling you for some time Fergy.
Fergy	I know it has.
Molly	This has interrupted your studies, surely . . .
Fergy	Oh yes—yes . . .
David	Surely at this stage in your studies you must choose percussion or brass . .
Fergy	I've chosen—I've chosen . .
Molly	Good, oh good—would you like to tell us?
Celia	I think it's important that he tells us his decision.
Molly	I do.
Celia	The group—all of us . . .
Fergy	Percussion.
David	Well done.
Fergy	I can't stand the noise.
	The Colonel laughs
	This may be only a temporary phase—when—that is—the drum beats were driving me mad—a sort of—I'm sorry—an insistent rhythm—bang bang—bang bang bang . . .
Colonel	But why study percussion?
Fergy	I can't like the brass—not enough—wind—I s'pose . . .

David	Woodwind...
Fergy	No...
David	Strings...
Fergy	*(shaking his head)* No—no...
Colonel	Have you ever thought about anything else apart from music?
Fergy	It's too late—you see—I'm sorry...
Molly	Go on, Fergy...
Fergy	My father has backed me to the hilt—I can't let him down—I'd rather be a bad percussionist—I don't care—if my head aches—all right it's an occupational hazard—why shouldn't I suffer—many do...
Celia	Oh, I feel for you Fergy...
Molly	So do I.
Celia	Oh, my head aches for you...
Carter	Head?
Celia	What?
Nurse Bryant	Perhaps Mr Carter thinks that another part of your body is more likely to ache?
Carter	I spoke quietly to Fergy last night—he has decided he wants to be a milkman.
Fergy	Yes—I feel it would be right for me—a service...
Carter	He can't tell his father—but surely Fergy, this is the first step in following up your decision.
Fergy	I'm frightened—I confess...
Parks	Perhaps you could go on, Fergy...
Fergy	Well, say—I get my father to accept—and then he trains me as a milkman...
Carter	The dairy would train you Fergy.
Fergy	Never mind—it might be the rattling of the bottles in the crates—next... So I should see it out in percussion—the devil I know...
David	I think you did well to speak of this Fergy—perhaps you could test paper bags—by putting your head inside them.
Colonel	*(smiling)* If noise is a problem perhaps you need a silent job.
David	A grave digger...
Fergy	Frankly—silence makes me nervous...

CAPTAIN OATES' LEFT SOCK

Parks	I think we all feel that Fergy is gathering himself for a big decision.
Celia	Good luck, Fergy—we all have to make one sooner or later—that's why we're here.
Fergy	Thank you—Thank you . . .
Carter	David was showing some aggression to, Fergy, I noticed.
Fergy	I noticed that.
David	Decide—decide—we've all got to decide—can't you see that—a group—decide what—as a group—decide the whole thing's a washout—no hope—eh—while he sits there—*(referring to the Doctor)*—like a buddha—the silent god—from whom the sparks of the ECT treatment may fly—look at him—like shouting to the skies—the heavens—no answer—what the hell's wrong with us—why are we here—silence . . .
	Silence
Celia	Are you getting nervous?
David	No-man's land . . .
	Silence
Carter	Perhaps William could explain his feelings about the group—we never seem to hear from him—or Rose . . .
	William does not answer
David	He won't help . . .
Carter	Why is that they—he—never speaks—perhaps he feels above it all—perhaps he feels the group is for morons—like us—he doesn't need it—then why is he here—pray—why—why? . . .
David	Food and shelter . . .
Carter	It could be more cheaply provided elsewhere—we have a trained staff—thousands spent—and yet William will not avail himself of any help.
David	Why not, William?
Carter	Why not, William?
David	At least the Colonel sleeps during group meetings—it seems a more positive act than your attitude . . .
William	I don't . . .
David	What?
William	See the point . . .
Carter	Why are you here?

William	It doesn't matter—why—why—go anywhere else?...
Carter	People are trying to get help here—people need here—good heavens, are you trying to tell us you don't need help—that you are above us...?
Nurse Bryant	It seems you don't like William.
Carter	Good heavens—why should he be so high and mighty—I know I need help—and I know I'm not going to get it—but to sit there smugly...
Molly	I think it is known that William and Rosy were working in a staff canteen—at the local bus depot...
David	Suddenly the buses run late—half the drivers and conductors ill—then they turn up—the two of them...
Carter	Are you suggesting they poisoned the food?
William	I—have no interest in the transport system...
David	Were they accused...
William	Food—fuel...
Molly	You think food is fuel?
David	He's trying to break down the municipal organization in this town—why? That was a working class canteen—were you wrongly accused?
Molly	Oh now, there was no evidence...
Carter	If they were guilty they should be prosecuted—if not why stay here—let the fuss die down—go somewhere else—
Nurse Bryant	Mr Carter did not answer my question?
Carter	I beg your pardon?
Nurse Bryant	About Celia's body?
Carter	Why am I supposed to have this absurd interest in Celias body? Heaven only knows...
David	Perhaps Nurse Bryant would prefer you to have an interest in her body.
Juliet	Or in your own...
Carter	I am being put upon—I feel it—not that I mind—that's why I'm here—losing out—but at the same time there is— group responsibility—say what you like to me.
Juliet	You are a swine.

CAPTAIN OATES' LEFT SOCK

Carter	I was waiting for that.
Juliet	So nice—like thin ice...
Carter	Thin ice, thank you....
Juliet	Pretty—but god save the child who ventures—out...
Carter	Are you referring...
Juliet	Oh shut up—don't be so bloody nice.
Carter	I am just not bloody hysterical...
Juliet	Then why—why—ask me out for an ice cream last night—me of all people—stick your ice cream—you're an old lech—you're an old boozer—frankly you're finished.
Carter	Do you think I need you to tell me that—ice cream apart...
Juliet	Always boasting about suicide...
Carter	Well now...
Juliet	Shut up—you haven't the guts—to kill a sow.
Carter	Now this is interesting—it's Juliet that's upset—my god—am I supposed to pretend to be nasty to satisfy her?
Juliet	God will punish me—he doesn't need your help—whatever you pretend to be...
Nurse Bryant	Juliet seems to be—upset
Rogers	She is probably upset for other reasons..
David	What reasons—what reasons?
Rogers	Ask Miss Cadish?
David	Why the hell should I? It's you that's got this secret reservoir of information—Nurse Rogers—Nurse Rogers—that use the group for your multitudinous purposes outside—that male nurse Rogers is always reassuring the girls in your corridors...
Rogers	Those corridors are National Health corridors—part of the hospital—they are not my corridors.
David	Leave her alone—I don't trust you...
	Silence
Parks	It seems that the question of trust is disturbing the group.. can any of us trust the group. I think that's enough for today..
	The Group rise to indicate the end of the meeting.

Fourth Group Meeting
All are present except Rogers
Silence. Juliet looks very upset

Molly	Juliet looks very upset today—perhaps she'd like to tell us why she's so upset—perhaps she would . .
Juliet	No . . .
Carter	If she doesn't want our help, then we can't make it available.
David	Where's Mr Rogers today?
Nurse Bryant	Its his day off.
David	Bully—I hope you report back.
Nurse Bryant	What?
David	We don't want him to miss any advantage—he'll be the first to go . . .
Carter	The first what?

Silence

Parks	Are you upset, Juliet? Perhaps you can tell the group why you're upset.
Juliet	No—no . . .
Molly	Only if we can help you Julie—it might help you to tell us . . .
Juliet	Oh no . . .
David	Quite right—anything you tell me I'll use against you—I'll blackmail any of you outside—so be careful what you say—I can get you outside . . .
Carter	David seems to be intent on threatening the group . . .
Colonel	Oh—you know—I think it might be his way of talking—he seems upset because Juliet's upset . . .
Carter	Why should he be?
Celia	Oh oh—why not—its natural—I don't hold that against him—if he can't control it . . .
David	What?
Celia	Your feelings—perhaps you know what's upsetting Juliet.
David	Society—bad meals in staff canteens—murderous toad in the hole—corridor meetings—brief glimpses of power—they're coming to take her away haha . . .
Carter	She seems no madder than the rest of us.

CAPTAIN OATES' LEFT SOCK

David	Abortion . . .
Carter	What?
David	Oh, come on . . .
Carter	I don't quite understand you . . .
Celia	I just want to help—anybody—can I—Fergy, I'd like to help you—on your decisions—and anybody—anybody—the best I can . . .
Nurse Bryant	You are fidgetting, Mr. Carter . . .
Carter	I beg your pardon. Oh yes, true—true—how true—I do need help—but I recognize that I can't get it—I'm sorry—I don't want to demoralize the group and any help you can give—to each other—I want to help—that at least I can do—Julia here . . .
Juliet	Ohh . . .
Carter	Juliet . . .
Juliet	Belt up—what do you know about the condition you'd like to be in?
Carter	I don't understand you, Juliet.
David	She is saying you'd like to be a pregnant old queen.
Carter	Oh that's it—oh I see—oh, it doesn't annoy me—you saying that—I mean, honestly, anything may be true of me—of myself—I've lost interest—anything you like . . .
David	That's a way of avoiding the issue.
Carter	I beg your pardon?
David	Truth is discrimination—if everything is true about you, nothing's true about you—comes to the same damn thing . . .
Carter	It's you that's name calling—go ahead—if I may use my tenure on life—to help a bit—oh I know it's only experience that comes with age—yes, age . . .
David	We can see your age—you don't have to boast about it—like some Peter Pan.
	Silence
Molly	I feel that Juliet might feel happier if she could tell us a little something—get it off her chest . . .
Juliet	No . . .
David	Why the hell should she?
Parks	You seem to implicate yourself in Juliet's problems, David.

David	It's nothing to do with me.
Celia	Oh Juliet, can't we help you?
Carter	I don't think it's any good pressing her too much.
Celia	I only asked her . . .
Fergy	I'm sorry . . .
David	What for?
Fergy	Eh? No, I didn't mean to interrupt—I'm sorry . . .
Parks	Perhaps Juliet can put her problem to us in her own words
David	You say that—you're the problem—you create her problems then ask her to state them—you—society—the sane representative—get off—it's like dropping somebody in a snakepit and asking them why they're frightened ..
Colonel	Is it fair to blame society on the doctor?—I mean surely we're all part of the same society—why blame the doctor . . .
David	He's in charge—or he should be—it's so difficult to blame him with the attitude he takes up—non-commital—it's like being a bloody waiting room—waiting for a trip . . .
Carter	Do we take it, Juliet, that you are pregnant—the word has got round—I don't know how . . .
David	It's amazing what you can pick up in the laundry room ..
Carter	I only said that to break the ice.
David	That's a change for you—how did you know she was pregnant?
Carter	Now be fair, I didn't—but to be fair—quite fair—Julie's pointed remarks to me left me with no other conclusion.
Nurse Bryant	What were they, Mr Carter?
Carter	It was suggested more or less—more than less—that I knew nothing about the state I would like to be in—pregnancy.
David	Was pregnancy mentioned?
Carter	It didn't need to be—I mean it was obvious—the way it was said—or the way it was understood—no you don't need to say that—I'm a jump ahead of that sort of remark—it's just that if I feel a thing I may feel a reason to speak out. Juliet . . . ?

CAPTAIN OATES' LEFT SOCK

Juliet	I am pregnant.
David	She didn't have to tell you.
Juliet	That's all right—now...
David	If any of you—oh...
Carter	You're speaking like the father.
David	I think she should have an abortion.

Celia bursts into tears

	'Course I'm not the father—I've only just met her..
Molly	Are you really pregnant, Juliet?
Juliet	I don't know...
Nurse Bryant	Celia seems upset.
Celia	No—go on—oh go on—please—its nothing.
David	She might not be pregnant—eh—a tissue of lies—but they're taking up definitive positions...
Carter	Who?
David	The doctors.
Carter	Have you been pregnant before, Juliet?
Juliet	Three times.
Carter	Oh...
Molly	Ohhh—don't worry...
Celia	*(sobbing)* Oh dear—oh no—don't worry—I'll be all right...
Juliet	I don't know—I don't know—they said I had children—how should I know—how the hell should I know.. it's nothing to do with me...
Carter	If you have children?
Juliet	It makes no difference to me—use my body—why should I know—I can go on—children or no children—it's all the same to me—don't bother me—use me—but don't please don't bother me...
Celia	*(sobbing)* Oh dear—dear—oh dear...
Nurse Bryant	Celia seems very upset—Mrs. Thompson...?
Celia	Abortion is evil.
David	Are you against it?
Celia	I didn't say that—one must always make allowances...
David	Always?

Celia	Oh yes—yes ... *(She sobs)*
David	Why should one make allowances if it's evil?
Celia	We're only human—God—God—God made us in his own image ...
Carter	Ohh ...
Celia	What?
David	Eh?
Carter	Only a small point ...
David	What
Carter	How could god have made us all in his own image?
David	You mean you and Celia?
Juliet	Easy ...
	Silence
Parks	Perhaps Juliet can explain what she meant by saying she didn't know whether she in fact had the children.
David	Children ...
Juliet	Three ...
Carter	You are not sure whether you had three children?
Juliet	Why should I be? I'm not interested, really I'm not—I have other interests ...
David	They might have been virgin births.
Carter	That shows a great familiarity with the holy ghost.
Juliet	I am not interested—the doctors ...
David	Have told her that she is pregnant again ...
Juliet	Why should I believe them—why should I—why did I believe them at all—at all—have I the children?
Celia	There are ways of telling—there are—oh dear—memories—I'd rather not remember ...
Juliet	Why the hell should you—it might be all brainwashing ...
Carter	Lady Macbeth ...
David	Can you believe what happens to while it happens?
Juliet	No—not yet—oh I'm not sure—perhaps I did—but who'll take my word—nobody else will—why should I ...
Molly	I'm sure we only want to help.
Juliet	Oh no, you all hate me ...
Molly	We don't—ohh no ...
Juliet	You must do, or how am I punished?

CAPTAIN OATES' LEFT SOCK 25

Carter   If you are punished you must believe in the crime—a crime? My dear Julie—I mean, heavens, to be fair—understanding—if you feel the need to be punished—surely it is you—you that have transgressed?

Colonel   Christ died for other people's sins (He laughs) Why shouldn't Juliet . . .?

Parks   And so on—and so on—perhaps I should have realized what was going to happen—I did in a way—didn't mean I could stop it—we're not gods you know—I have no authority to moralize—though being employed on society's behalf—that is—should I not serve the morals of that society—but it is precisely because these morals have broken down that they come to me—Quad Et Ratum—Nish Nash Nosh . . . I am not a moral force—I am not a destroyer of morals—I am a man who likes to keep my shoes clean—look here, we do try and keep 'em alive, you know . . .

Hospital Dining-Room

(Note: the following scene may be acted, or simply narrated as a remembered incident, by Parks. It is better to narrate than to break the spell of the group therapy room)

Breakfast time. Nurse Bryant brings in the mail. Carter gets a small package. He goes to his room, opens the package and takes out a plastic bag. He goes to his locker and takes out a new ball of string, takes a pair of nail scissors from a leather case and snips off a length of string. He puts the plastic bag and string in his pocket and goes down the passage into the 'Gents'. Fergy comes out of the dining-room, strides down the passage, stops in his tracks, deliberates determinedly. He turns and strides back up the passage, stops, turns, stares with determination at nothing, strides down the passage to the 'Gents' door, looks back up the passage, shakes his head, takes out a coin and spins it. Pleased with the result, he pockets the coin and confidently enters the toilet. There is a pause, then he rushes out and up the passage. He comes rushing back with Nurse Rogers and the Colonel. Up the passage the news spreads. They enter the toilet and drag out Carter, cutting off the plastic bag tied over his head.

Parks' Narration—in place of the above:

| Parks | The next morning our dramatic incident occurred. Fergy went to the toilets—being of indecisive ilk, he hesitated and spun a coin to see whether he should relieve his bowels before or after breakfast. Even a simple decision like this he couldn't make for himself without conjuring up another deciding factor—lady luck. Well, the coin came down in such a manner—heads or tails—that he was safe to proceed to the toilet. In a cubicle he came across Mr Carter, who had tied a plastic bag round his neck and was suffocating. Fergy rushed for help—without spinning a coin—which is worthy of note—and the life of Mr Carter was saved. The group assembled some time later . . . |

Fifth Group Meeting

All are in their places, including Carter and Rogers. That is, all except Doctor Parks, for whom they are waiting. Parks comes in, shutting the door, and sits down. Silence

Celia	Oh, somebody say something—I mean, surely someone can start the meeting . . . I mean ooh this silence—what's it mean—why can't we talk—I mean surely—this our treatment—oh dear—are we getting anywhere—really—are we—someone tell me—please?
David	All becoming a bit madder every day—be barmy time we leave here, if we weren't when we came in—are you awake, Colonel?
Colonel	Yes thank you . . .
David	Perhaps you would like to start the meeting—in the doctor's absence.
Molly	The doctor is here, David.
David	Is he? I can't see what difference that makes.
Rogers	Are you angry with the doctor?
David	What? Here we go in fear of our lives and he says nothing—nothing . . .
Roger	What do you expect him to say?
David	Count the dead—count the living . . .
Nurse Bryant	Who is frightening you—David?
David	The group—they demoralize me—you can't go round with a horde of suicides without becoming depressed—you lot—I mean when your're mentally ill,

CAPTAIN OATES' LEFT SOCK

	what's the good of mixing with a lot of insane monsters...
Juliet	The sick leading the sick...
David	Put out the eyes of the man that sees...
Molly	David that's hardly fair—surely—to call us monsters—we came here for help—this is a hospital.
David	Bloody abattoir...
Nurse Bryant	You seem upset, David, about Mr Carter's suicide attempt?
David	No—hell—of course not—those toilets aren't for suicide— they're supposed to be for natural functions—after breakfast—what a bloody time—inconvenient—he knows everybody's using the toilets after breakfast...
Nurse Bryant	You think Mr Carter chose a time when he would be discovered—hopefully...
Fergy	I'm sorry—really I'm sorry—that is, I feel I've created this disturbance—I was going to wait till after the group meeting—feeling this might be better— sorry...
Nurse Bryant	Better?
Roger	I think he is talking about discharging his bowel functions.
Fergy	Yes—that is—no—I felt I had to make a decision—regardless of the consequences—that is I had little thought of Mr Carter's suicide.
Carter	I don't expect you to calculate my distressed state of mind when going to the toilet—certainly not.
Fergy	I don't know though—surely—that is—in a decision—all the possible factors should be jumbled up—sorted out...
David	Have you in fact been to the toilet yet today?
Fergy	No.
David	Do you feel resentful against Mr Carter for this?
Fergy	Oh no...
Carter	I'm sorry Fergy, I seem to have bodged the whole thing.
Fergy	Oh no—no—that is—it was worth it.
Carter	Thank you.
David	What's a little constipation if it saves a human life...
Molly	David—aren't you treating this a little nasty—Mr Carter must have been very upset—very upset—and I think we're all very upset for him. I certainly am.

Celia	Oh I am—I am—when I heard—the news—I cried—I wanted to—do something...
Carter	I'm glad you didn't.
Celia	I would have...
Carter	There was nothing you could do.
Celia	For you—to think of another human being suffering—lacking comfort and warmth—that I might be able to give...
Carter	Celia, thank you, I did not lack your warmth—that has nothing to do with the case—the cause lies in the past—the miscalculation was mine—it would have worked—only when I got the bag in the morning post I was keen to get on with the job—to have done with it—I bear Fergy no malice...
Fergy	Thank you...
Carter	For answering the call of nature...
Fergy	If the coin had come down tails...
Carter	What?
Fergy	A weakness—forcing a decision upon myself...
Carter	I don't understand you.
Fergy	I had to toss the coin...
Carter	*(cutting in)* Never mind—let us leave it at that—please—I don't wish to discuss the embarrassing situation I have put the group meeting in—I apologize, it will not occur again—I expected to be out of your way—I had decided...
	Silence
Parks	It seems the group are much concerned with the need to make decisions today—perhaps this is all part of growing up—perhaps the Colonel could enlighten us on this often frightening process of decision making?
Colonel	To him who hesitates all seems possible—I suppose—and yet of course one gets nothing that way—and eventually I suppose—loses everything—you can't have everything—but if you make your decisions not only do you lose by deciding—but you gain something by embarking on a course of action...
David	Suicide?
Colonel	Mr Carter is not dead...
Carter	I'm sorry.

CAPTAIN OATES' LEFT SOCK

Colonel — Fortunately—sooner or later he will have to reject suicide—it seems to me—or—or live in terror the rest of his days. I'm sorry, I don't wish to butt in . . .

Carter — By all means . . .

Fergy — I think that time makes many decisions for us.

David — That's all very well for the bowel habits—with the help of a few sennapods—but surely we create time by making decisions—or else years drift by without meaning . . .

Carter — Precisely—I was trying to give meaning to my life by ending it—it seemed about the only positive thing I could really achieve—without harming other people . . .

Parks — Would you care to elaborate that statement?

Carter — I beg your pardon?

Parks — If I hear you—correct me if I'm wrong—you feel that—that you can make no other decisions—than suicide—with harm to other people—people you're fond of perhaps—or may grow fond of . . .

Carter — Yes Doctor, that is the case.

Parks — Does this not bear on fears you may that—that only too easily you could repeat—a painful experience that happened before . . .

Carter — Indeed, that is true—rather than that—rather than risk that—I will end it all—I think it is fairer—anyway it is for a man to decide whether he would rather destroy himself than other people.

David — Captain Oates.

Carter — Precisely.

David — I wonder what really happened.

Carter — What? I beg your pardon?

David — We only have Scott's word for it—it must have been almost unbearable inside that tent—the group . . .

Carter — The group . . .

David — The group . . .

Colonel — *(laughing)* Oh come now, are you destroying a national myth?

David — Captain Oates feet may have caused a lot of concern—they might have—frankly he might have been asked to leave the tent—and take his socks with him—they were never found you know . . .

Carter	I can assure you that my feet are washed every day—twice a day...
David	Then the responsibility rests with you.
Rogers	Aren't we getting a little away from the point—about decisions—can we not make decisions—for instance, Mrs Topps cannot make a decision about her discharge from the hospital.
Molly	I look to the doctor to do that—I think its only fair...
David	And yet Mr Carter here will discharge himself from this planet—without the doctor's permission—without even God's
Carter	God doesn't enter into it—I would rather bear any punishment than hurt anyone else.
Juliet	Oh yes—yes...
Carter	For once Juliet agrees with me.
Juliet	Oh yes...
Carter	If they won't nail us up, Juliet, then we'll have to do it our-selves.
Juliet	I feel I have been nailed up—and I'm glad—I don't mind if it will put an end to somebody else's suffering.
Nurse Bryant	Who did you have in mind Juliet?
Juliet	I beg your pardon?
Nurse Bryant	Whose suffering could you see yourself relieving? The world's?
Juliet	Oh no—no. I'm not that arrogant—just perhaps—I don't know—one or two.
Carter	Your parents...
Juliet	I suppose so.
Carter	Why should it give them pleasure, Juliet, to see you suffer?
Juliet	It does—it does—it must do—or else why would they do it? *(she buries her face in her hands)* THE GROUP wait I don't mind—really I don't...
Celia	We're here to help you, Juliet—that's why we're here—surely your mother and father don't really want to hurt you—my mother hurt me—oh, she did—she did—so much—but she was ill—she was almost demented—and all she could see to hit out at was me...

CAPTAIN OATES' LEFT SOCK

Juliet   Yes...
Celia   I'm sure she regretted it—sometimes—at least...
David   Did she ever tell you she regretted hurting you?
Celia   No—what's that mean?
David   Then she might not of—perhaps some people feed off pain...
Celia   If theyr'e ill—surely only if they're ill.
David   Well, there's plenty of pain in the world.
Carter   Why add to it—Juliet...
Juliet   I feel it's called of me—that I deserve it. I do I know I do—I must be punished—for what I've done.
Carter   But don't you, Julie, start off with this desire to be punished—and then commit the acts to satisfy yourself—acts that you feel justify punishment—acts that may outrage your parents...
Juliet   I suppose so—oh, I don't know...
Parks   We seem to be making some headway here—wait a minute—if I may sum up—if I may...

    Silence

Mr Carter would commit suicide to avoid hurting other people—and Juliet—Juliet would punish herself for other people—to bring her parents together, perhaps...
Juliet   Yes...
Parks   They both—Mr Carter and Juliet—seem to share a concern for other people's welfare. But I wonder—I wonder are they really doing—behaving in a way that is best for other people. Thank you, that's all we have time for today.

Dr Parks gets up and exits. The others drift out

David and Fergy stack chairs

David   Bastards—bastards...
Fergy   What?
David   If it's pain they want, they'll get it—they'll get it.

David and Fergy exit

    INTERVAL

Sixth Group Meeting

All the Patients and Nurses enter, arrange the chairs and sit in the circle

           Dr Parks enters and joins them

Silence

Molly   David, why did you come in here?

David   I was terrified—I was full of panic—I couldn't breathe—I felt unless I concentrated, my heart would stop beating—I'd get paralyzed—die—I don't know . . .

Molly   What were you frightened of?

David   That I'd kill myself—not that I'd want to—I think too well of myself for that—why shouldn't I—but—we all have our moments of weakness—not like Mr Carter—he wants to kill himself—and can't . . .

Carter   I will.

David   I want to stay alive desperately—but can't—I mean I can—but it means guarding against an irrational act—I can't cross a bridge—I might jump over it—I might go under any bus or car—just one weak moment and I'm out and under—sometimes I can't shave in case I cut my throat . . .

Carter   But people are crossing bridges every day of the year.

David   Them—what do they know? It never enters their minds that they could jump—over—the trouble is it's tiring—being on your guard—one gets tireder and tireder until—you can fight it no longer—have done with it . . .

Parks   It seems that like Mr Carter—David has a feeling to kill himself.

David   Not like him—he won't go through with it.

Parks   You're both still alive—excuse me for pointing that out.

Carter   Yes, how true . . .

David   It's just an idea that's crept up on me—like some secret fascination—a dare—almost—why? Perhaps I'd like to attempt everything.

Carter   Everything—that's interesting . . .

David   Oh yes, you'r going to say I'm a suppressed homosexual—I don't want anything to do with it—it appeals to me sometimes—yes I have a desire—but I like women—that is sexually—what's wrong with that . . the more the better . . .

Celia   Why do you want so many women? I'm sorry—I'm curious, David.

CAPTAIN OATES' LEFT SOCK

David	Well, because they're there—why does a man climb mountains? It's a challenge . . .
Rogers	Do you feel challenged by anyone in this room?
David	What?
Rogers	Male or female?
David	I don't so much feel a challenge with Juliet—attraction yes—it would be easy . . .
Juliet	Yes, I s'pose . . .
Carter	That's bloody arrogant, if you'll forgive my language— I would regard her as a definite—a—a definite . . .
Parks	Challenge?
Carter	No I don't feel that any more—not since the baby died— I feel more protective—and I don't think that a statement . . .
Parks	But excuse me—forgive me—but didn't Juliet say something . . . Yes I s'pose—to David's declaration of attraction . . .
Carter	Oh yes, well, we're all cooped up in here, aren't we . . .
Parks	You feel cooped up?
Carter	My God, I could let my hair down—but we are ill—we the sick must not become dependent on each other—it would be fatal—to form a relationship—an attachment— in here—surely this is hospital policy—against degrouping — it is so easy for two people to detach themselves from the group.
Parsk	Precisely—there are extensive grounds for that sort of behaviour—acres—but surely self restraint . . .
David	Who do you think fancies you?
Carter	I beg your pardon?
David	Easy for you to practise restraint—if there's no opportunity—unless you contemplate rape . . .
Celia	Oh David, surely every dog has his day.
Carter	Thank you . . .
Celia	I mean . . .
Carter	Don't mention it, Celia . . .
Celia	You are an attractive man—to some . .
Carter	Some—yes—the old and the blind, I suppose—it doesn't matter—this is nonsense—as you know, Doctor Parks, I had a very strong attachment with a girl who left here—but I wouldn't dream of degrouping— although she was most attractive . . .

David	There's no rule against it—is there—if Juliet and I want a bit of degroup one night in the old grounds—well is there a rule—in this damn place—what—we'll only discover the rules by breaking them . . .
Rogers	Do you think it is clever to take advantage of someone in a distressed state of mind—assuming you could with any of these girls? I'm sure they're decent . . .
David	What the hell do you think you're running—a convent? I'd degroup with the bloody lot of 'em if I had my way—I could degroup about three times a night—and then come back for a quick hive off . . .

The Colonel laughs

David	This group loyalty is carried too far.
Molly	What do you think, Juliet—about what David says?
Juliet	Oh, I don't know—probably—that is I don't blame David—not at all—he is distressed—if I can help—oh well, I suppose I would . . .
Carter	A real angel of mercy—a pregnant one at that.

Juliet buries her face in her hands

	I'm sorry Juliet—that was only said with the intention of helping—of protecting you—and David . . .
Juliet	I know—I would be wrong for him—I know. I'm wrong for everyone—but what can I do—there's some people I feel I can help—might be able to . . .
David	Men—people you're attracted to—would you like to help Mr Carter?
Juliet	I couldn't—I'm sorry . . .
˙Carter	That's all right—I didn't ask you for help, Juliet—certainly not of that sort—I would not dream of taking advantage . . .
David	She's already said you haven't a bloody chance . . .
Carter	All right . . .
Celia	It takes all sorts to make a world—and I feel Mr Carter has a right to his—oh, his own desires . . .
Carter	Thank you Celia—my desires are quite dried up—since . . .
David	Since what? What? I've yet to hear this . . .

CAPTAIN OATES' LEFT SOCK

Carter	You have not been here so long as some . . .
Fergy	I'm sorry . . .
Carter	Fergy—knows . . .
Fergy	Yes—I don't blame your wife either . . .
Carter	No, she was utterly distressed—poor dear—poor dear—I forgive her—now—it takes time . . .
David	What did she do, rape you?
Carter	She took the life of my baby—she well—put a plastic bag over the baby's head—two months old—I tried the kiss of life but it didn't work.
David	Oh—why did she take the baby's life?
Carter	I think she loved him too much—couldn't bear for him to be hurt—so killed him.
Fergy	You had a very special relationship with your wife.
Carter	I know I did, Fergy—and I must say in five years of marriage—this is the only incident we ever had.
David	*(laughing)* The only one! My God . . .
Carter	It's not a bad record.
David	My God—are you mad?
Molly	David . . .
David	Must be—that's why he's in here—and they let you out at nights.
Molly	David—his wife could have had a brainstorm—five years of good marriage—
Carter	Lovely, idyllic years . . .
Molly	are not thrown away for nothing. I have had a wonderful marriage . . .
David	And I've had a bloody awful one—but the kids are still alive. What was so special about your marriage?
Molly	It could have been a brainstorm—I'm sure it was—no premonition . .
Carter	None—I kissed the baby good-bye and went to the office—home for lunch—but she—well—you know—she was hanging out the baby's nappies when I left . . .
David	The sun was shining . . .
Carter	I believe it was . . .
David	Oh, get knotted!
Molly	David . . .

Celia	I'm so grateful that tragedy has not struck in my house .. it's been hard enough—bad enough—without tragedy.
Fergy	It could have been a brainstorm . . .
Carter	Yes . . .
Fergy	But my own impression . . .
Carter	Go on . . .
Fergy	I feel—I have decided—quite firmly in my own mind—about that situation—that—I don't want to hurt you . . .
David	That you don't want to hurt him?
Fergy	No—yes—that firmly—she was frightened you'd leave her.
Carter	I had special arrangements with my girl friends I told you that—this was all arranged before we got married—she knew—my nature . . .
David	Ha . . .
Carter	My nature—she was not like that—one man was enough for her.
David	Where did she find him?
Carter	Very clever—five happy years—and I tell you in all modesty she was satisfied—oh she was—yes without a doubt—without a shadow of a doubt—not often—but when she was she was—perhaps . . .
David	What?
Carter	The fact that—a young man like that wouldn't understand this . . .
David	Go on.
Carter	Her joy . . .
David	Her joy—go on.
Carter	Would last for months . . .
David	Years . . .
Carter	Months . . .
David	Till she screwed herself for another production.
Carter	I don't understand you.
David	Was she in Equity?
Parks	David is suggesting are you not David—that Mrs Carter may have been acting the part of being fulfilled.
David	Yes, they call it the sexual act don't they?

CAPTAIN OATES' LEFT SOCK

Carter	You may say what you please—it may help—I don't know—the group—I'm only talking about it at your instigation—it can make no difference to me—my mind is made up . . .
David	Is your wife in another hospital?
Carter	That is the case.
Colonel	Any change of you being re-united?
Carter	None—I shall never see her again.
David	In heaven maybe—with the baby . . .
Carter	David—you'll only upset yourself going on like that.

Silence

Celia	I have decided to divorce my husband. I thought I should let the group know.
David	She is now available for limited seasons in the hospital grounds.
Carter	Oh, bully!
Celia	Divorce is a serious business—please—tell me if it isn't—it's what I've been taught . . .
Molly	And what will happen to your five children, Celia?
Celia	Well, it's one less to look after isn't it—with Roddy my husband . . .
Carter	Without Roddy your husband . . .
Celia	I feel sorry for him.
Carter	Yes . . .
Celia	Seriously I do—oh really—I cried last night—I was his anchor—something he could always come back to—however far he strayed—I kept a home going— a warm bed—oh really I realize it's all wasted now—he came home less and less—took me and the children for granted—there we were . . .
Carter	Why do you think he was reluctant to the bosom of the family, Celia?
Celia	Oh, he said he didn't like the children in bed—I slept with the three of them.
Carter	The youngest . . .
Celia	The oldest . . .
Carter	What the small ones might have got crushed—I'm sorry—I had an image—unforgiveable . . .
Celia	I got so lonely—how could he expect me at five in

	the morning to kick the wee children out—to make way for him smelling of drink . . .
Carter	Crumbs between the sheets . . .
Celia	What Mr Carter—please advise me—am I being evil in letting the man go?
Carter	When did you last see him, Celia?
Celia	Six months ago—oh five months . . .
Carter	It's hardly a case of letting him go.
David	So he caught you in bed with the children . . .
Celia	Last time he was home—there's only two rooms—we're sort of cramped together—we sleep in the living room and the children in the bedroom—like—the baby in with us—the cot—and the four kiddies in the small bedroom—we tried it the other way round . . .
Carter	Pardon?
Celia	But it was so difficult to entertain . . .
Carter	Quite. Oh yes . . .
David	A few friends back for coffee—don't sit on the children . . .
Molly	Oh it's so sad—it's so sad—I think it's very wrong—there shouldn't be a housing problem.
Carter	I agree—but the more space we provide—never mind—I agree—wholeheartedly.
Celia	So he stayed out—late—very late . . .
David	What, late into the autumn . . .
Carter	Some years . . .
Molly	Mr Carter . . .
Carter	I'm sorry—I really am—I realize a serious problem—David was egging me on . . .
Celia	I know I shall never find another man . . .
Carter	He'd have to be a small man, would you say . . .
Celia	What?
Carter	The limited accommodation—look here, I'm sorry Celia—I realize I'm being facetious—it's most unlike me . . .
Parks	In Celia's case, Mr Carter, you fight shy of regarding her problem seriously?
Carter	Thank you doctor. I suppose I do?

CAPTAIN OATES' LEFT SOCK

Parks	I wonder why? Why would we fight shy of other peoples' problems?
David	We don't want to get involved—better to have a laugh . . .
Carter	I can see no question of involvement with me and Mrs . . .
Celia	Call me Celia—you always do—please—Harry.
Carter	Harry—yes . . .
Celia	If you don't mind . . .
Carter	No,no,no—I am quite unamazed—that is I am of service . . .
Celia	That's what I felt about you.
Carter	To the group—to the group in general—call me what you will—discuss anything—to all intents and purposes for myself—I have ceased to exist.
David	Then it really doesn't matter what Celia does to you?
Carter	I beg your pardon?
Parks	One moment—one moment—do you remember—in an earlier meeting—now Juliet described the same feeling—of wanting to be used—shall I rephrase that . . .
Carter	Please . . .
Park	Now—let me put it this way—an atittude of submission perhaps—though in Juliet's case it was submission only to certain people—whereas Mr Carter—forgive me . . .
Carter	Please go on Doctor.
Parks	Seems willing to make himself available for the whole group.
Juliet	He reminds me of Celia—in a funny way.
Carter	Go on—Juliet—we might as well hear it.
Juliet	Oh the availability—I could see you—oh no—yes I could—sort of rolling—lying in bed surrounded by a brood . . .
Carter	Charming—well we give you full marks for imagination, Juliet—though precisely what it means I don't know. I certainly could not see you in bed with your children—impossible as they've been adopted in their various ways . . .
	Juliet buries her face in her hands
	I'm sorry to upset you—I did not mean to be bitchy . . .

Juliet	Oh no, no—it's true—it's—oh it's some awful punishment. I deserve it . . .
Carter	It might be easier your way.
Juliet	What—oh, tell me what you like.
Carter	It might be harder to keep the brood around you in bed—than distribute them at random and then complain about being punished . . .
Juliet	I know, I know . . .
Carter	It seems you may be getting the best of both worlds, Juliet
Celia	Oh, the children are a blessing—I couldn't be without them.
Juliet	I know—oh—I am aware of that.
Celia	You see, I love them—I do—I suppose I can do without Roddy . . .
David	There's not much room for him.
Celia	No, not really . . .
David	Unless they lowered him from above on a crane—for a limited season.
Carter	During the mating season—I'm sorry . . .
Celia	Oh, I like my problems being discussed . . .
Carter	I wish I could bring more purpose to your problem, Celia.
Celia	Oh I'm sure you can . . .
Carter	And where are the four children now?
Celia	In homes?
Carter	Homes—good . . .
Celia	They're having a lovely holiday—then—well it isn't so bad—I might—the doctors said—the welfare people are trying to get me a house.
Carter	A council house?
Celia	Yes—where—oh, it will be a relief—and of course Roddy will have to keep paying . . .
Carter	Roddy will have to keep paying . . .
David	For five careless moments—it's not exactly what you would call—expect of a marriage . . .
Celia	He was a good man—very ,kind to the children—when he was home—though of course he got irritable to

CAPTAIN OATES' LEFT SOCK

	them—he—oh, he always started off nice—but oh there wasn't room for him to be nice really.
Carter	What did he say the last time he left?
Celia	He said, 'I'm just popping down to get some milk from the corner shop' . . .
Carter	I see . . .
Celia	You see one of the children was ailing . . .
David	Were they all Roddy's children?
Celia	Oh yes—yes yes—I was a—yes—yes . . .
Parks	Was a . . .?
Celia	Virgin . . .
Carter	When? I imagine we were all virgins once. Except Juliet . .
Juliet	Oh I feel sometimes I'm still one . . .
Carter	Yes, I can't see it applies in your case . . .
Juliet	Still . . .
Carter	Yes, at . . .
Juliet	Oh five weeks overdue—six—no seven—but I still can't believe it—why should I—the doctors tell me— so it's up to them . . .
Parks	I'm sorry, Juliet—can you explain that remark— possibly?
Juliet	Oh well—it's you that say I'm preggers, isn't it.
Parks	Yes.
Juliet	So—I mean—I wouldn't concern myself—I mean it's up to you.
Parks	You disown responsibility for your condition?
Juliet	What condition? I don't feel any different.
Parks	But . . .
Juliet	I never did—anything—any time . . .
Parks	But—am I right, Juliet—in saying that you described— your second pregnancy—sorry, your second delivery of the baby as a long painful one?
Juliet	It might have done—it really doesn't matter today— the sun is shining through the window . . .
Carter	Juliet, it seems you are running away from the truth of your situation.
Juliet	What does it matter?

Carter	What? I beg your pardon?
Juliet	Oh all right, go on at me—I know I deserve it—if you go on at me there must be a purpose—to punish me . . .
Carter	Is it right that the doctors have told you that you should abort this time?
Juliet	Yes—oh I don't care—you must do what you want to me—I am to be punished I know that—you choose—any way—I don't care—you make me suffer—your way. I was only trying to help.
David	Who?
Juliet	All the lame ducks . . .
Parks	Can you describe that further?
Juliet	Well—oh—it seemed to me—that it was the only way I could help them—do anything—was to oh—give them my body—I suppose—at the time . . .
David	Did you expect pleasure from this?
Juliet	No—it was part of my punishment.
David	What?
Juliet	For going with them—I couldn't expect to get off scot free could I—I don't I don't—I expect to pay—that's why I'm here . . .
	Silence
David	Why should you be punished—why not enjoy life?
Carter	But if she enjoys being punished—which seems to be the case . . .
Juliet	I don't know—really . . .
David	There's Dorothy over there—locked in silence punishing herself—all right, darling?
	Dorothy smiles at him and nods
	Everything's all right—don't worry—are you coming out to play today? We're having a lovely time—it's a game without consequences—makes a—makes a change . . .
Celia	We don't know much about you, David.
David	It's quite simple—my wife prefers to be screwed by other men.
Rogers	Screwed—do you have to use that word?
David	Screwed.

CAPTAIN OATES' LEFT SOCK

Rogers	That word—does it please you to be needlessly offensive?
David	What?
Rogers	There are ladies present.
David	So what—what's screwed—they get her in the hedge, mate, and whip her knickers down and give her a good seeing to—or in the back of the cars mate they poke her till they're fed up then drive her home—screwed—screwed rotten—shut up—ladies—sod the ladies—get knotted—get stuffed—get screwed, the lot of you! You—you're a protector of the ladies are you—'cos you can't get your little bit of shufti—make sure no-one else does
Rogers	Now look here . . .
David	You make me sick.
Rogers	If only you would stop acting.
David	Acting?
Rogers	Oh yes—acting—all these shock tactics . . .
David	That's what I feel.
Rogers	It's not how it comes over—it seems to me you are more concerned to shock other people than examine your own feelings.
David	Right, right, I like her being screwed—I play with myself thinking about her being screwed by other men—right—get stuffed—I'm fed up with it—and I'm play acting aren't I—get knotted—I'm acting I have no feelings—I'm sick and tired of the whole bloody thing—I've come to hospital to have a bit of degrouping—get away from all the rubbish . . .
Molly	Why do you think your wife goes with other men, David?
David	Revenge—no—I don't know—she likes it—likes it—I can't stop that can I—I like going with birds—all right.
Rogers	Then why get upset?
David	All right, I suppose I love her.
Rogers	But you go with other—birds . . .
David	You got to—got to keep the flag flying. It's different for a woman—well I suppose its not—logically—socialistically—it's fair—sleep round where you like—

	both partners—equality—it's fair—that's why I'm in hospital—I hate her—long live equality—I'm sick—equal screws for women—I'm ill—excuse me—Utopia has arrived—I'll just throw myself over the nearest bridge—Screw! Let me out of here . . . *David jumps up and heads for the door. Doctor Parks and Nurse Rogers rise.*
Parks	David . . .
David	Away, away . . .
Parks	I think the group would appreciate it if you would stay with us. *David, near tears, stops with his hand on the door knob*
David	What's the point?
Molly	We would like you to stay David.
David	Why?
Molly	Well, we don't like to see you rushing off like that in such a distressed state.
Carter	I think we all feel like David sometimes—like just running out—I think I would if I had said what he had—I understand.
David	It's an act—just a bit of acting.
Carter	I would say not.
David	Well, tell that monstrous male nurse . . .
Rogers	David—I only spoke as you came across to me—I think your distress is real now—if you could sit down and tell us perhaps we can help.
David	Oh yes—part of your scheme, isn't it—break 'em up—work out the way to do it—how much do you plan . . .

David returns to his chair. Silence

	I don't know why I got in this state—it seems to me incredible—not that I trust you—the group—you can't help me—what are you going to do tame her desires—if I kill her that should stop her—I've come damn near it . . .
Molly	Did you say you had children, David?
David	Two—oh they witness most things—surprised she doesn't take them out with her lovers for the joy rides—anyway it gives me freedom—I can do what I like—no holds barred—screw—I always have done—

CAPTAIN OATES' LEFT SOCK

	but had to fight her morality—her jealousy—old fashioned—there's nothing to fight now—that—but it's got to be kept under the carpet—she couldn't forgive me that—broadcasting the news—what are we frightened of—sex—creeping round the town—screw—everybody knows about it—say nothing—drunks talk—weep in their beer—and the avenging angels go about their screws—I was drunk flat out by evening—she's just tarting up for out—charming—well it's what I wanted—what she wanted—see what she wanted—at least I can trust her—trust her to screw—bitch...
Parks	Do you feel your wife is morally wrong?
David	No—perhaps—I am morally wrong—and she is—but it doesn't seem so important when I'm morally wrong because at least I can go back and be forgiven—it's hopeless—like a fornicating church—like a priest with a choir boy in his side of the confessional while you rabbit on—like—bread and cheese and pickled onions two milk stout some old newspapers and a baby's rattle—meaningless—rattle...
Molly	Are you religious then, David?
David	No, I hate religion—I know—that I might have the psychological structure of mind—you know the old religious bit—somewhere—probably I worship fanny—excuse me, Mr Rogers—her fanny—fanny, stuck for want of an old Anglo Saxon word...
Rogers	Aye...
David	It seems a last refuge—an escape—I don't know—the corruptible womb—refuge here—join the queue—lovers to the left—have you a ticket, sir—I'm her husband—giggles down the queue—what's it matter—I can get it elsewhere—somebody else's missus—get your own back—somehow—I hate happily married couples—they are corruptible...
Molly	Is your wife beautiful?
David	Yes—I'd prefer a pigface—that's how she looks to me anyway—like a greedy pig—greedy for revenge—rucking—in England's green and pleasant land—let's talk about something else.
Juliet	Are your children happy?
David	Its all for the children, isn't it—that's what keeps

	us together—together, ha—till I get enough strength up to return and murder her—this time . . .
Juliet	I think you'r making a mistake—I'm sorry—from what I know of you—sounds a bit hopeless . . .
David	Why should it be—why should I give in . . .
Parks	(to the audience) The next morning was deceptively quiet to begin with . . .

Seventh Group Meeting
Silence. Silence

David	Well, as no-one else is saying anything I'd like to complain about the occupational therapy facilities—I mean over the weekend—they're non-existent.
Nurse Bryant	And yet you fell asleep during occupational therapy.
David	That was during the compulsory period—why we should have to moon round making baskets and trays like bloody idiots I don't know—anything more calculated to make you feel infirm . . .
Molly	I think David wanted to play table tennis over the weekend.
David	Yes.
Carter	There's been some trouble . . .
David	What?
Carter	Bats stolen—store broken into—not us, of course . . .
Molly	Some time ago . . .
David	So we are to be punished for other people's sins.
Fergy	They don't trust us.
David	I don't trust them—but we've got to live together on this planet.
Nurse	Supervision—I think that's the problem—over the weekend there's no OT staff to supervize the store . . .
David	Are the facilities—are they run for the convenience of the OT staff or the patients—this is our place for the weekend—you lot—doctors—OT people—bugger off to your own lives—it's then we patients have a chance—we're left alone—but because we're not supervised we can't play table-tennis—what am I going to do, eat the balls? Stick your OT . . .

Rogers	Do you think it is unreasonable for the staff to have a weekend off?
David	You can have the whole bloody year off as far as I'm concerned—you're not doing anything for us—why not leave us to run the bloody hospital—you've got your own lives—you come and feed off us for your bloody livelihoods—make us feel like animals in some zoo . . .
Rogers	You're allowed out over the weekend.
David	Allowed—allowed is it—have the surrounding district been warned to stay indoors—who allows us?
Rogers	There is no restriction over the weekend.
Molly	It's very boring—nothing to do . . .
David	No rules to break—no compulsory OT to sleep in—can't get off . . .
Celia	We don't seem to stay together as a group over the weekend.
David	What?
Celia	There's too much pairing off—and some of us are just left . . .
David	What are we going to do—tie ourselves to each other . . .
Fergy	I've noticed that—over the weekend people drift apart—it may not be a bad thing—it's certainly lonely . . .
David	Listen, if you want us to stay together—we need a sacrifice—a ritual murder—a ritual murder to tie us together in guilt and remorse—none of this private self-punishment thing—we do it together—batter one of the OT staff to death with table-tennis bats—you make me sick—the group—why do we need the group—we cheat—we are ready to form a group—a virile something group—instead of peeping out of our bloody neurotic minds—at each other—shall I screw Juliet on the carpet in front of you—a communal action of sorts—you complain about degrouping over the weekend—all right, what do you want us to do—do it in front of you—are we prepared to go the whole hog and form a group—instead of just rabbiting on—sick . . .
Nurse Bryant	See you saying that . . .

David	That I hived off with Juliet on the grounds over the weekend—and what wicked purpose would that encourage on your behalf—she's already preggers—so what . . .
Molly	Surely, David, in her emotional state . . .
David	Her state? What about my state? My needs? I could be going mad for it—what—getting the cold bit from Agatha the star whore of my home town whose husband pays for every bloody round—then come here to play bloody table tennis all day—all right let medicine advance—this place should be a bloody brothel that's what we need, eh Celia?
Celia	Oh well—I mean I don't know about modern medicine—I'm against brothels . . .
David	But if the treatment prescribed for you by the doctors was a good'un—say a mutual seeing to—you and Mr Carter . . .
Carter	Oh come on . . .
Celia	Oh please . . .
David	But if the doctors prescribed it would you?
Carter	They're hardly likely to prescribe medicine of that sort . . .
Nurse Bryant	Do you like medicine?
Carter	I don't . . .
Celia	Oh—oh—oh dear—oh dear Mr Carter I'm not a pill . . .
Carter	I realize that Celia—and I wouldn't take you, believe me . . .
Molly	Oh dear—dear, dear David, you do say such things . . .
David	Perhaps you could be prescribed—might prescribe the Colonel . .
Colonel	*(laughing)* Yes—I should have a very lucky doctor . . .
David	It's you that's getting it, not the doctor . . .
Rogers	Would you really like to have sexual intercourse in front of the group?
David	Corr blimey, here we go—do you know a joke . . .
Nurse Bryant	We take everything seriously here—even jokes.
Parks	To discover what people mean?

CAPTAIN OATES' LEFT SOCK

David	Do you want me to flash it—do you—do you—do you—just say the word—do you want me to flash it do you—do you—do you—eyes down for a full house eh—come on, what's the matter with you—bloody jokes—I'm not joking . . .
Parks	I think David is saying—that is asking one of the group—to ask him to exhibit his sexual organ.
David	That's it yes, you got it—come on—any offers—come on then—once in a lifetime this . . .
Carter	Go on then, young David, flash it.
David	Eh?
Carter	Come on then—if that's what you want.
Rogers	I say . . .
David	You shut up—there . . .
	David flashes it. Reaction
Molly	Oh no—no, no . . .
Celia	Oh David—David please . . .
Rogers	*(jumping up)* We don't have to put up with this—stop that immediately.
David	Yes, so much for your bloody rules, mate—treat us like chimpanzees we'll act like em . . *(Doing his trousers up)* Look at that fraud over there—you'd like to, wouldn't you, mate—you might be in here for that for all I know—no guts, eh—its nothing . . .
Molly	Doctor this has gone too far . . .
Rogers	I agree . . .
Celia	I must say so . . .
Molly	Surely, surely—we should not be subjected to this—I've come here to get well.
Celia	Yes, yes . . .
Molly	I only wanted my date of discharge and David—oh David, how could you . . .
Rogers	There is such a thing as the hospital management board . . .
David	Oh, you go and flash yours to them, mate—leave me alone—gutless wonders—no sense of bloody humour have you—so I'm sick, am I—sick of you lot . . .
Molly	David that's dreadful, how could you—to us—your friends . . .

David	Keep it amongst your friends, mate.
Parks	David—now hold hard a minute—let us get this thing in perspective. David—David...
Molly	You shouldn't allow that sort of thing in your group meeting doctor.
David	That's right, let the patients lay down the bloody law—it's mob law that's all. (Pointing at the Doctor)With that coward presiding—you're a mob—a mob—and I shall treat you as a mob.
Parks	This group—
David	Mob...
Parks	does not take very kindly to your exhibition. Was it your intention David to antagonize them?
Colonel	He didn't antagonize me—rather foolish perhaps—ladies, etcetera—but quite harmless.
David	Thank goodness there's one person here—and even he's got me worried...
Margaret	I think that this should be reported.
David	I wondered when you'd speak again—at least Dorothy isn't accusing me, are you girl—all right—there's nothing wrong is there?
	Dorothy shakes her head and smiles at him. She unclutches her hands then clutches them together.
	Look at that—look at the way her hands moved—bring a little joy to some people—prudes...
Parks	A mob, you said, David—but the Colonel and Dorothy—as well—she seems not to disapprove of your action...
Molly	Oh, she can't speak for herself.
David	She bloody well can—she's done it.
Molly	Your language—oh my...
Parks	Are you against that part of the mob which is for you?
David	Certainly not—if there's enough of us we'll carry the day.
	Margaret, still very upset, runs out
	The meeting breaks up
Parks	*(to the audience)* Well, young David had certainly put the cat among the pigeons. Secretly, I was

CAPTAIN OATES' LEFT SOCK

pleased. I couldn't let this be known—I expected results—and by heaven I was getting them. I looked forward to the next day . . .

Eigth Group Meeting

The Patients and Nurses settle down again. William, Rose and Margaret are no longer with the group.

David	Our numbers are depleted.
Molly	Margaret has gone home—she was quite firm . . .
David	After complaining to the hospital management board—bully—and the young ones—Hansel and Gretel—they've been whisked away to another ward—so we wait for the axe to fall—not that they can do anything—to me—to me—but I came here to get away from threat—doom—but there's no let up—is there, Doctor?
Parks	You are saying that you feel threatened?
David	'Course I bloody well do.
Parks	You want me to reassure you.
David	About what?
Parks	Perhaps you can tell us.
David	Balls . . .
Molly	David . . .
David	Who stood by me—in my hour of need . . .
Molly	You were wrong—very very wrong.
David	Wrong . . .
Molly	It set me back—I was ready to be discharged—now I feel the sooner I get out of here the better—its altogether different.
Fergy	May I—that is—I'm sorry . . .
David	Mmmmmm . . .
Fergy	I feel I should have demonstrated with you—I—I've decided—but I don't think it would help to take my trousers down now.
David	No . . .

The Colonel laughs

Fergy	I can make decisions—but they always seem too late—or too early. I have a letter here—*(He shows a letter)*—received yesterday—unopened—I can't decide whether to open it or not—that is—perhaps—no no . . . *(He puts the letter away)*

Carter	Are you trying to say, Fergy—
Fergy	Yes, I am.
Carter	that you lack the confidence to open letters away from the group?
Fergy	No—no,no—perhaps it's a matter of deciding—the long term effects—why are they still writing to me—me—us...
Carter	They should write to us.
Fergy	She...
Carter	She would write to us...
Fergy	Perhaps it would be quicker—I don't know—yes—yes...
Carter	You think she doesn't know about us.
Fergy	She wouldn't care...
Molly	Surely—surely—the group is to give us strength doctor to go away from the group—into the world—to face ourselves—our responsibilities..
Celia	That's how I see it—I shall never forget you—all of you and David...
David	And David—and old Uncle Tom Cobley and all.
Fergy	No I mean... *(He takes out the letter, waves it about)* Yes..
Parks	Do you want to open the letter and read it to the group?
	Fergy puts letter away again, distressed
Carter	Have you lost the confidence to read your own letters?
Fergy	Yes, yes—to be honest—no I—I thought—read the ruddy letter just before the meeting and rush in—but say—say—I ran the wrong way—the letter may...
Carter	Have that effect on you?
Fergy	Yes...
Carter	You could perhaps read the letter quietly just in the presence of the group...
Fergy	*(taking the letter out)* Thank you—thank you—*(He hesitates. Then opens the letter. Reads it. Puts it back in the envelope. Puts it away)* Thank you. She wishes to know whether she can have her record-player back—yes, it's the key—to my digs—not the fact she's pregnant—she could have the key—the player—I mean—I don't feel I can marry her.. I have decided

CAPTAIN OATES' LEFT SOCK

	that I am the father—I have decided to tell my father—but she wants the player back—never—never—either one thing or the other—if I'm the father why should she want the record-player back...
Carter	She might want to play it—Fergy.
Fergy	Fergy—yes—can't she wait—has she got no trust?
Molly	The letter seems to have upset you—Fergy?
Fergy	Take the key—take the flat—take the player—take the baby—take all the responsibility...
Carter	You feel that she is trying to move her things out...
Fergy	Why? I said I was the father—I decide—damn the player...
Celia	You're distressed, Fergy—you think she's leaving you—you might not be the father.
Fergy	If I am how can I prove it—I—I—I was only with her one night.
Molly	Do you love her?
Fergy	I can't stand the noise—the noise—I would marry her and send my career crashing into ruins—but to have the ultimate decision thrown in my face...
Carter	She doesn't want to marry you? Perhaps she is thinking of your career...
Fergy	I hate my career—it's so noisy—just imagine sitting in the middle of a bloody orchestra—the din is incredible—that's apart from my own noise—I lose control—I bang the drum—drown 'em out—a single violin, I can't stand that even—bang the drum—bang the drum—drown her out...
Carter	Does she play the violin?
Fergy	I—that is.. *(He stands. Takes the letter from his pocket. Tries to eat it. Spits it out)* I wish I'd taken my trousers off—I wish I'd taken a stand with David—why am I always too late—late—I'm not going out there again...
Carter	Sometimes—doctor—I feel we get worse in here—not better.
Fergy	Yes, yes... *(He sits down again)*
David	What do you expect? Out there—they're carrying on their own lives—untrustworthy, vicious—then they have the cheek to visit us—I know—how they upset—these

vicious hospital visits should be stopped—half the inmates in tears when they've finished their condolences—what's wrong with us—prove it—prove it—don't just stare at us—some dumb show—you're not so bloody clever—the lot of you—we came from you lot—and we shall return to you—in force—united . . .

Fergy   Yes . . .

Molly   Doctor—surely you could let me know my date of discharge . . .

Ward Corridor

(Note: the following scene may be acted, or simply narrated as a remembered incident, by Parks, as before)

Morning. Fergy comes up the corridor with some unironed washing and goes into the laundry room. From further up the corridor he is watched by Dorothy, but does not notice this. He comes out of the laundry room with a pile of neatly ironed gear. Dorothy watches, and quickly looks in the laundry room. Then she runs after Fergy and leaps on him, pulling him to the ground. Laundry scatters, amongst it a pink bra. Dorothy makes funny grunting noises as she pinions the slight Fergy down with her weight. Other women come and help her—and some of the chaps appear on the scene. Fergy is pulled to his feet and confronted with the evidence.

Parks' narration—in place of the above:

Parks   Almost like a war—you cop it when you least expect it. Margaret's letter to the management board about David flashing it—enclosing measurements, no doubt—pardon—had filtered through the channels. *(He takes out an official-looking letter)* And got back to me. *(He puts the letter away again)* And so, as the sun rises every morning, we gathered in our cheery reception room to talk once more amongst ourselves. Nurse Rogers was hardly speaking to me these days—which I approved of—but I did get the grim news that it was Fergy who had been taking the girls' undies from the laundry room. Dorothy grabbed him. The matter would now be subject to debate—but I knew that day—matters wouldn't end there. I too would have to break my silence that day—like a bolt from heaven—I would choose my moment—or at least I cared to think so . . .

Ninth Group Meeting

Fergy is absent, and there is a Newcomer, a slight, nervous man whose fears have seized him up so that he walks with a stick

CAPTAIN OATES' LEFT SOCK

Juliet	Well, what a lovely sunny day it is—it makes one feel good to be alive—well, not quite—where's Fergy?
	Fergy comes in late. The Newcomer is sitting in his chair, so Fergy reluctantly sits elsewhere
Parks	You were saying that you find it a lovely day Juliet—would you like to explain that to the group—I mean your feelings of—would happiness be too strong a word . . . ?
Juliet	No certainly not—I do feel happy—very happy—I feel like a pink bra . . .
Parks	A pink bra?
Juliet	Oh yes—a lovely pink brassiere—its a lovely feeling—it gives you such uplift. *(She laughs)* If you could become your clothes—oh it's been done, surely . . .
Fergy	I—that is—feel no shame—I was acting under instructions . . .
David	Who from?
Fergy	*(indicating Carter)* Well . . .
Carter	Oh now, Fergy—certainly I will take the blame—you have a life ahead of you . . .
Fergy	It's not that . . .
Carter	But are you denying you took the bra?
Fergy	I took it with you in mind—I decided—that is—so useless—do something for someone—David here—he does—so I took the bra for you—yes . . .
Carter	Why me?
Fergy	I don't know—it was a decision . . .
Carter	Fair enough—if taking things is making your mind stronger . . .
Fergy	For you . . .
Carter	Forever—you might as well embark on a course of shoplifting—each article will represent a decision taken—who knows one day you might be a great politician . . .
David	You've got to start somewhere . . .
Juliet	It's such a lovely day—has no one noticed how the sun is shining.
Molly	It's hot—very hot—uncomfortable.
Juliet	Oh, I don't know . . .
Fergy	I feel sorry . . .

Carter	Go on . . .
Fergy	Not enough—respect has been taken—for my action—action.
David	Certainly—did not we hear Dorothy crying for help—and the word was made flesh—then the flesh was made word—help—well done Dotty. *(He waves at Dorothy)*

Dorothy smiles and waves back

	We have a considerable force at our disposal—on watch at all times . . .
Colonel	I would be interested—that is to know why Fergy thought Mr Carter—sorry—*(laughing)*—needed a pink bra?
Fergy	Yes—thank you—to me—I thought what else does he need . . .
Carter	I want for nothing—nothing.
Molly	But that was my bra Fergy—was that not very naughty of you?
Celia	It was Molly's bra—if Mr Carter wants a bra he has only to come to me and ask . . .
Carter	Thank you . . .
Celia	Not at all—I want to help you.
Carter	But I didn't send that little—angel of mercy to steal a bra for me.
Juliet	What a beautiful day . . .
Celia	Oh no—no—but who took the slips?
Fergy	They're in his locker. *(To Carter)* No, I mean they're under his mattress—I mean I looked in his locker and they weren't there.
Carter	They weren't there . . .
Fergy	Under your mattress—I decided to look.
David	Perhaps Mr Carter kept the slips under his mattress to keep the wrinkles out of them.
Carter	I know nothing.
Parks	Let's get this straight—are you Mr Carter—forgive me—denying all knowledge of the slips?
Carter	To be honest, I knew they were there—though to be frank—quite frank—as to how they got there—that I also know—I did put them there for safe keeping.
Molly	Oh, Mr Carter . . .

CAPTAIN OATES' LEFT SOCK 57

Carter	Girls can be very destructive—my wife left her things lying everywhere—even when she was out shopping . . the place was littered with her underwear—and its supposed to be my day off.
Parks	Can you explain that remark a little?
Carter	No.
Parks	Very well.
Carter	I got into the habit of tidying up—tidying up—I suppose in the laundry room it struck me—the same . . .
Celia	My slips—my slip—oh Mr Carter—was hanging there to dry.
Carter	It was dry before I removed it.
Celia	Thank you.
Carter	It is quite safe, Celia.
Celia	Oh I know it is—if only I'd known—one needs a man about the house I've always said that—to tidy up—I'm such a scatterbrain.
Carter	Count the children . . .
Celia	Oh yes . . .
Carter	One—one gone . . .
Celia	So many . . .
Carter	You have so many—one wouldn't notice one more or less—that's the attraction—one wouldn't notice—one crushed—one suffocated—one more or less—even if it was me . . .
Celia	Oh Mr Carter—please don't take on.
Carter	No . . .
Celia	About—oh those pink things—I can always have some more . . .
Molly	Mr Carter has been sick—very sick—and he shouldn't trouble about the slips—of course Margaret before she left complained about her slip gone missing . . .
David	And my indecent exposure—perhaps the doctors had word . . .
Parks	A patient is free to write to who he or she wishes—that is—the case.
David	Did you take my part?
Parks	To be honest—which I am to you—the hospital board is holding an emergency meeting today.

David	To discuss my future...
Parks	Margaret has threatened to go to the press unless action is taken.
David	I'm glad she's back on her feet and operating in the outside world—I'm glad I did that for her—and you—you I suppose are quite ready to cast out the sick...
Parks	Do you think so?
David	What did you do? Make it a matter of confidence? Well, I am going—I am not willing to wait for the moralizing considerations of the committee—I was told morality didn't enter into cure—that is treatment here—not till its damn well convenient—you can't shut us off from morality in here unless we bloody well do what we're told—there is no respite—why pretend—you—doctor—play your little game—hateful—when the crunch comes—out...
Carter	You seem convinced of the doctor's attitude—can you not see that you may take the consequence of your actions—even in here?
David	You beastly transvestite—you dishonest scoundrel—you getter at getting at other people to do all the dirty work..
Carter	Go on—you can't hurt me...
	David rises and picks up his chair
David	I'd bang this in your bloody face...
	Carter cowers behind Celia
	Come out from behind your ever-reproducing whore...
Celia	Leave him alone—anyone who harms Mr Carter harms me...
	David collapses in laughter before Rogers and Nurse Bryant can disarm him. The Colonel laughs
Colonel	Very good.
Rogers	I must say you go too far.
	David pushes Rogers in the chest, sending him staggering
David	Get off—this is group therapy—anything goes...
Rogers	No...
Parks	No—the group must be considered—David—you are part of the group.

CAPTAIN OATES' LEFT SOCK

David	I am the leader—don't talk to me—there's been a palace revolution mate...
Rogers	I think that until David has been removed we should abandon this meeting doctor.
Parks	All right Nurse—sit down a minute.
David	You won't abandon me—I'm abandoning the lot of you.
Parks	Are you declaring an intention to leave us?
David	That will solve your bloody problem won't it. *(To Juliet)* Are you coming?
Juliet	Oh yes—it's such a lovely day outside...
David	Come on...
Parks	Now hold on—are you declaring an intention to discharge yourself David?
David	Yes, and I'm taking my little degroup with me.
Rogers	You have no right to that girl...
David	Shut up, you jealous fink.
Rogers	She is unwell—in our care...
David	They're all voluntary patients in this ward, mate—she can go when she pleases—with who she pleases—she's over twenty-one—we all are—why should we wait upon some obscene hospital board—is that how you run your cures?
Parks	There is no cure—that I have spoken of...
David	You won't stand by the bloody group, will you—you bastard.
Rogers	I'm warning you...
David	Shut up.
Rogers	I have had enough of this—Doctor I feel I must report this carry-on immediately to the hospital board in session—I have my rights as well—though no-one seems aware of them—even nurses have rights...
David	You have the rights and I'll have the birds—ha...
Rogers	That girl is pregnant—the question of her abortion and future has yet to be decided—by us.
David	By you?
Rogers	By us.
David	What about the group?
Rogers	You may discuss what you like.

David	But you take all the important decisions.
Parks	No-one is forced...
David	They're all still brainwashed in your pernicious way, aren't they...
Juliet	It's such a beautiful day..
Newcomer	What is all this about? Excuse me, I'm new here...
David	Group therapy.
Newcomer	You're allowed to hit people with chairs in group therapy?
David	Anything...
Parks	No—the basis of group therapy—Mr...
Newcomer	Parks.
Parks	That's my name as well.
Newcomer	No, that's my name—oh come on—that's the group is it—pinch your name—you the doctor are you—I doubt it—where's your stethoscope! I came here to be cured not to be hit by chairs—I demand protection...
David	My father left me a barn—that is land—he was a gentleman—who never exposed himself—except on his own property—extensive acres—he could walk naked for miles—this barn I converted into a gang headquarters—some time ago—on the moors...
Juliet	It would be so lovely on the moors today...
Parks	*(taking out his letter)* The hospital management decision I have—here—it came through before the meeting—our last meeting...
David	No...
Parks	In this particular case—I'm sorry—the future of group therapy is endangered—by the carry-ons here—I don't moralize...
David	If you did moralize what difference would it make—your'e on the same bloody side.
Parks	What is one group—there is a whole future in this branch of medicine—I'm sorry—simply said—this group could give a bad name to the whole future of psychiatry—a la group—we have just begun...
David	Yes we have begun—but you are too cowardly to go on.
Parks	Most of you will be dispersed to other groups.
Newcomer	What other groups? Where are they taking me?

CAPTAIN OATES' LEFT SOCK

Parks	Some may be fit for discharge.
Molly	I would so much like the date of my discharge, doctor.
David	Perhaps you should discuss it with the group . . .
Parks	I'm afraid it's too late for that—I mean—that is—if it means anything to you—forgive me—I am retiring from the medicine—the official body—the NHS—not to go privately—the whole body of medicine recognized today—I'm sorry—I can stomach no more—I—I must apologize for being so definitive . . .

> *They all move to the audience, leaving Parks alone. Now the Patients have become spectators, like the audience.*

(*To the audience*) So they all took off to David's father's estate—of all things—en group, so to speak—and I—I have decided to join them.

> *Nurse Bryant goes to Parks*

Nurse Bryant?

Nurse Bryant	I'm coming with you—I couldn't abandon you . . .
Parks	To the moors?
Nurse Bryant	I believe in you.
Parks	I'd rather you believed in my methods . . .

> *There is a pause, then the group come back from the audience and welcome Parks—and Nurse Bryant—as if he has come to them. Rogers—who has switched his loyalties—now shakes hands with the Doctor again. Rather belatedly, he starts singing 'For He's a Jolly Good Fellow', encouraging the others to join in. They do so.*

FURNITURE AND PROPERTY LIST

On stage: 14 small chairs

Personal: Carter: cigarettes, matches, ashtray
Fergy: letter in envelope
Parks: official letter in envelope

The following properties are required if the events outside the clinic room are acted instead of narrated:

Mail (letters and packets) including one containing plastic bag
Ball of string
Scissors in leather case
Coin
Pile of ironed washing
Pile of unironed washing, including pink brassiere

LIGHTING PLOT

Property fittings required: nil

Lighting should be uniform and general, with no changes whatever. House lights should remain on throughout.

www.ingramcontent.com/pod-product-compliance
Ingram Content Group UK Ltd.
Pitfield, Milton Keynes, MK11 3LW, UK
UKHW021842140426
5217IPUK00022B/1554